GREAT GRILLING & HOT SAUCES

Other Schiffer Books on Related Subjects

GRILL SKILLS
Professional Tips for the
Perfect Barbeque: Food, Drinks,
Music, Table Settings, Flowers
ISBN: 978-0-7643-4768-9

DUTCH OVEN
ISBN: 978-0-7643-4218-9

**THE LITTLE
SMOKER BOOK**
ISBN: 978-0-7643-4772-6

Copyright © 2015 by Schiffer Publishing, Ltd.

Library of Congress Control Number: 2015931311

Originally published as *Das Geheimnis der Grill &
Chili Saucen: Zutaten, Herstellung & viele Rezepte*
by HEEL Verlag GmbH, Konigswinter © 2014 HEEL
Verlag GmbH.

Translated from the German by David Johnson

Photographs by Fabian Rapp

Original Layouts by Christine Mertens, Heel Verlag

Type set in The Sans, The Serif & Disintegration

ISBN: 978-0-7643-4851-8
Printed in China

Published by Schiffer Publishing, Ltd.
4880 Lower Valley Road
Atglen, PA 19310
Phone: (610) 593-1777; Fax: (610) 593-2002
E-mail: Info@schifferbooks.com

For our complete selection of fine books on this
and related subjects, please visit our website at
www.schifferbooks.com. You may also write for a
free catalog. This book may be purchased from
the publisher. Please try your bookstore first. We
are always looking for people to write books on
new and related subjects. If you have an idea for a
book, please contact us at

proposals@schifferbooks.com.

Schiffer Publishing's titles are available at special
discounts for bulk purchases for sales promotions
or premiums. Special editions, including
personalized covers, corporate imprints, and
excerpts can be created in large quantities for
special needs. For more information, contact the
publisher.

Tips & Recipes

GREAT GRILLING & HOT SAUCES

Ralf Nowak

4880 Lower Valley Road • Atglen, PA 19310

CONTENTS

CHILI SAUCES

GRILL & BBQ SAUCES

FOREWORD

My consent came spontaneously, perhaps a little too spontaneously. When the nice lady from the Heel Publishing Company asked me on the telephone if I could imagine writing a book about grilling and hot sauces, I wasn't entirely certain what this would entail. True, it is my hobby, my passion, my occupation, and I know a lot about what makes an outstanding sauce. But write a book? A little product knowledge, a few examples, recipes, general information—with your knowledge it shouldn't be a problem observed the editor. And then I said yes, even to a nearly impossible deadline, without knowing what the great chili spirit had in store for me.

The idea that the attitude of editors towards preparing grill and hot sauces was the same as mine was also not helpful, now that I had in front of me a book project that I was supposed to drag-and-drop between my sauces. But a yes is a yes and it is a well-known fact that a man grows with his tasks.

One cannot go unpunished for thinking up sauces with the names "Hot Mamas" and "Painmaker," which have gained a considerable market presence, and it is not without consequences that one is on the road as the "Painmaker," selling these two sauces. As a trained cook and master chef, I can look back on thirty-eight years of experience, and during this time my enthusiasm for "hot sauces" has steadily grown. My greatest concern is to pass on my experience and knowledge about chilies and the making of chili, grill, and BBQ sauces in a simple and understandable way. I gladly accept the opportunity and, in this book, allow myself to show you the ropes. In the process I betray more than a few of the secrets that I have learned about the chili over the years.

Enjoy browsing, trying the recipes, and, of course, eating!

Ralf Nowak

PREPARATION

It is important to consider a number of things before setting to work. Here are the most important points:

Please remember to wear proper protective clothing when working with chili peppers, read the first-aid instructions, and prepare an emergency kit—which will surely be used.

This may sound excessive, but it is based on my own experience, for I know of no one who has not sat in the corner gasping for air with burning eyes during a first attempt at making sauces. The cleaner, calmer, and more concentrated one works, the better. As long as it looks and tastes good, nothing can go wrong.

If vinegar is needed, always use your favorite type with an acid content of between five and ten percent, whether apple, wine, alcohol, malt vinegar, or another kind. The choice of chilies is up to you. In the tables that follow you will find suggestions as to which chili is right for which taste.

One should use salt just as sparingly as types of vegetable that are a strain on the body, such as onions, cabbage, mushrooms, and root vegetables. In terms of digestibility, it is better to cook chili sauces than to use them uncooked.

FIRST-AID

IF CHILI GETS IN THE EYES

Stay calm; don't react frantically. Whatever you do, don't rub your eyes with your fingers.

WHY SHOULD ONE USE OIL AND NOT WATER?

The substance capsaicin in chili peppers is fat-soluble; therefore, the oil can wash the capsaicin out of the eyes. This is not possible with water. One rubs the capsaicin in even more and then spreads it, but it is not removed. As a result, the pain becomes worse and lasts longer. In case of doubt one should always consult a doctor.

THEN THE FIRST-AID KIT COMES INTO PLAY

It consists of: paper tissues or paper towels and a bowl of vegetable oil.

If the eyes are burning, because chili has got into them as a result of rubbing them, for example, one should take the following steps:

Drizzle plenty of vegetable oil on a tissue and wipe the painful spot on the eye. Note: if the pain is closer to the outside of the eye, rub outwards, if it is more in the direction of the nose, wipe toward the nose. One must only wipe *once* with the same tissue (Note: wipe and throw away). A fresh tissue must be soaked in vegetable oil for each wipe. After repeating this process three to five times, the pain should lessen noticeably.

INTERESTING FACTS ABOUT CHILIES

ORIGINS

Capsicum annuum originates in Mexico and northern Central America. South America is the area of origin of *Capsicum frutescens*.

SPREAD

In the sixteenth century, Portuguese and Spanish explorers brought the chili pepper from South America to Asia, where it quickly became part of the local cuisine. It subsequently spread over all of Asia.

PRODUCTION OUTPUT

At present, approximately 35 million tons of chilies are grown worldwide. Demand increases from 3.5 to 5% annually.

PRODUCTION OF THE CHILI PEPPER BY NATION
(as a percentage of the total)

China	56
Mexico	8
Turkey	7
Indonesia	5
Spain	4
USA	3
Nigeria	2
Egypt	2
Korea	2
Holland	1

Source: FAOSTAT

FACTS

The Importance of Chili in Hot Climate Zones:
The body reacts to hot foods by perspiring, which cools it. Chili peppers are, therefore, are very popular in warm and hot regions.

Chili as a Staple Food:
Along with the pinto bean, the chili is an official staple food in Mexico and New Mexico.

It is, therefore, no surprise that more chili peppers are eaten per capita in New Mexico than in any other state in the USA.

If it Burns:
Do not drink water or carbonated beverages. The pungent substance in the chili (capsaicin) is fat-soluble; therefore, it is better to drink whole milk. The fat in the milk dissolves the capsaicin and washes it away. Yogurt is also helpful.

The Characteristics and Causes of Pungency (Spicy Heat):
As a rule, the following principle applies: the smaller the chili, the spicier it is.

An alkaloid called capsaicin is responsible for the spiciness of chili and paprika.

Capsaicin is a colorless, pungent-smelling, crystalline compound with the chemical formula $C18H27NO3$. It has been suggested that plants developed capsaicin to deter natural enemies.

The Center of Pungency:
The hot part of the chili is in the placental tissue, which holds the seeds. The seeds themselves are not hot, but capsaicin is transferred from the placental tissue to the exterior of the seeds, which is why the myth still persists that chili seeds are hot.

The Worldwide Consumption of chili:
One in every four people on the planet eat chili daily.
That is 25% of the world population.

Chili and Health:
Chili and thus our well-known paprika are free of cholesterol, low in sodium and calories, rich in Vitamins A and C, and are a good source of folic acid, potassium, and Vitamin E. Chili contains more Vitamin C per gram than citrus fruits.

The Desire for Pungency:
The pain that is triggered causes the brain to release endorphins, the body's own morphine, to relieve it. This leads to a feeling of well-being and can even have a slight addictive effect. Endorphins regulate feelings like pain and hunger. It is linked to the production of sex hormones and is jointly responsible for the creation of euphoria.

Pungency and the Sense of Taste:
Spicy food does not negatively affect the sense of taste—quite the contrary. After a brief period of habituation, one perceives the various flavor nuances of food much more intensely. The sense of taste becomes more pronounced. Millions of Asians can't be wrong. Many good chefs also eat very spicy food.

Chili and Burning Pain:
It is not possible to burn or injure oneself with chili, even though it may feel that way. The pain is an illusion caused by the capsaicin. Capsaicin is a neurotransmitter and docks at the pain receptors in the mouth. These receptors suggest a "burn" to the brain.

Chili in Medicine:
Chili has been used as a natural remedy for many ailments for centuries. Chili peppers aid digestion, hamper the growth of some harmful pathogens in food, and improve the body's metabolism. The Mayans rub chili pepper on their gums to treat toothache and inflammation. The

Chili and Superstition:
In southern India, it is common practice to place chilies and a lemon above the threshold of a house to ward off evil. In Sicily, an amulet in the shape of a chili pepper is hung around the necks of newly-married men. Chili is said to prevent the wearer from being unfaithful.

Incas consumed chilies to improve their eyesight. In Mexico, chili peppers are prized as a hangover cure. Nowadays, conventional medicine uses chili to treat circulatory disorders, sore throats, muscle tenseness, and in various cancer therapies. The list is steadily growing longer.

Measuring Pungency:
In 1912, the American druggist Wilbur Scoville invented a procedure entitled "Scoville Organoleptic Test" to test the pungency of chili. The pungency is measured in Scoville Heat Units (SHU). Today, capsaicin content is measured by means of gas chromatography.

DEGREES OF PUNGENCY

CAPSICUM *Chinese*	
Over 1,500,000 Scoville	Trinidad Moruga Scorpion
Over 1,000,000 Scoville	Trinidad Scorpion
350,000–900,000 Scoville	Bhut Jolokia (aka ghost chili pepper)
350,000–550,000 Scoville	Red Savina Pepper
100,000–350,000 Scoville	Habanero Pepper

CAPSICUM *Pubescens*	
50,000–100,000 Scoville	Rocoto Pepper

CAPSICUM *Fructescens*	
50,000–140,000 Scoville	Bird's Eye Chili
2,500–10,000 Scoville	Peri Peri
1,000–30,000 Scoville	Tabasco Chili

CAPSICUM *Baccatum*	
15,000–30,000 Scoville	Aji Amarillo
15,000–30,000 Scoville	Lemon Drop

CAPSICUM *Annuum*	
30,000–50,000 Scoville	Cayenne Pepper
2,500–5,000 Scoville	Jalapeno
100–500 Scoville	Peperoni from Italy
0 Scoville	sweet peppers

Note: Scoville values are always determined from dried fruit.

The different degrees of hotness are divided into a scale from 0 to 10. The degree of pungency of the various chilis can be found on this scale.

CAPSICUM ANNUUM

This includes **sweet peppers**, which are not hot (pungency 0).

The **Peperoni** from Italy, the **Jalapeño** from Mexico, the **Cayenne** from South America, and the **Thai Chili** from Asia can reach a pungency level of 1 to 6.

Jalapeño

CAPSICUM BACCATUM

These chilis have a very intense aroma and emit a very powerful smell.

Among them is the **Aji Amarillo**, which achieves a 6 on the heat scale.

Lemon Drop has a pungency level of 7 on the heat scale.

Aji Cuencano rates a 7 on the heat scale.

Aji Amarillo

CAPSICUM CHINESE

This is the hottest pepper type in the chili family. Chilies of this kind are immediately recognizable by their incomparable smell. Anyone who has had it in his or her nostrils will never forget it. The various varieties are Habernero, Scotch Bonnet, Congo, and Seasoning Pepper.

The **Habanero Chocolate** is best known and is a 10 on the heat scale.

The **Red Savina Habanero** is a 10 on the heat scale.

Scotch Bonnet rates 10 on the heat scale.

Naga Jolokia or **Bhut Jolokia** is a 10+ on the heat scale.

Trinidad Scorpion, the newest variety, is a 10++ on the heat scale.

Habanero

CAPSICUM FRUCTESCENS

Peri Peri is 3 to 6 on the heat scale.

This includes the famous **Tabasco Chili** with a rating of 8 to 9 on the heat scale.

Tabasco Chili

CAPSICUM PUBESCENS

The most famous chili of this kind is the **Rocoto,** which reaches 6 to 9 on the heat scale.

Rocoto

As this type contains black and dark brown seeds, I do not recommend it for Caribbean-style sauces, as the dark seeds do not look appealing. Gardeners should be aware that the varieties hybridize quickly, passing undesirable traits on to other varieties of chili.

A CHILI EXPERT'S INSIDE STORY

Not everything sold in the supermarket as chili powder or chili flakes is actually chili as you would expect it to be.

One must be aware of the following: industrially-manufactured (ground spices) are ground and packaged in large halls within mills. If dried chili is ground, other mills and spices become contaminated with the pungency of the fine chili dust. To prevent this and to keep production costs to a minimum, nature lends a helping hand:

Normal, non-pungent red sweet peppers from the *Capsicum annuum* family are ground or processed into flakes. They are then moved to a remote part of the building. There the pepper powder is placed in a large mixing drum and is sprayed with *Oleoresin capsaicin* (natural chili extract). The mild pepper takes on a wonderful red color and also becomes hot, depending on the intensity of the spray. It is actually impossible to distinguish powders visually. Flakes can be, however, for in nature no one chili flake is like the others. Industrially-produced chili flakes all appear to have the same color and, when eaten, the industrial flakes still have a certain "sweetness" on the

tongue. The only real sign of authenticity is the price. True chili powder costs several times more than the industrially-produced product and the list of ingredients precisely specifies the type of chili used. When shopping, one should also pay attention to the percentage of chili, for cheap products can be stretched up to 70% with salt, sand, ash, and cellulose.

DO SAUCE MAKERS CHEAT WHEN IT COMES TO THE SCOVILLE VALUES OF THEIR SAUCES?

This question is not easy to answer. When one considers that the Scoville value often determines sales numbers, each manufacturer obviously tries to achieve as high a Scoville value as possible. I know no one who prints the Scoville value on the bottle. These Scoville values are usually made public by Internet shops. As a rule, the figures are somewhat optimistic for, normally, no one has a gas chromatograph in his kitchen to check the numbers, and there are very few who can recall the painful experience of true 100,000 Scoville. My experience shows that most are exaggerated many times over (up to a factor of 10). This does nothing to spoil the overall effect, however, for these sauces are unspeakably hot, even if they do not reach the specified values. A guide is always offered. Claims specifying heat levels of 1-10 or 1-20 are more honest, for they allow the user to prepare for what awaits him. Unfortunately, exaggerated heat levels and sensationalism, as well as the forbidden passing of extreme extracts to the end user and the use of unauthorized ingredients, such as chemically-pure capsaicin, have led to a tightening of the regulations. The federal states and the EU are now addressing the issue of how much heat should and can be expected by the consumer. Hopefully, this will not result in our one day having to choose from standardized heat levels.

RECIPES

The degree of
difficulty in
preparation is
indicated by ⊛

⊛ ☆ ☆ ☆ ☆ ☆

very easy

⊛ ⊛ ⊛ ⊛ ⊛ ⊛

very difficult

CHILI VINEGAR

This is the simplest way of making a chili sauce yourself—quick and always successful. The vinegar is especially well-suited for seasoning. The result is especially original and decorative if you use a nice bottle or other glass container.

Ingredients

Makes about 1½ cups (250 ml)

About ⅔ cup (100 g) fresh chili, variety according to taste

About 1 cup (200 ml) vinegar, at least 5% acidity

Secret Preparation

In principle any chili can be used. One must bear in mind, however, that the color of green chili changes within twenty-four hours and becomes quite unappealing. Red, yellow, or orange chilies, on the other hand, retain their lovely color for a longer time.

First cut the chilies into decorative rings, strips, or cubes, which look better in the bottle. Then place the chili pieces in the bottle until half full and add vinegar to about ¾ inch (2 cm) below the rim. Then seal the bottle, but not airtight, and allow it to rest in a dark space (i.e., a refrigerator or kitchen cupboard) for 10 days.

After the rest period, the simplest chili sauce in the world is finished. One can vary the flavor by adding cloves of garlic or herbs. After use, the bottle should always be sealed and stored in the refrigerator.

CHILI OIL

Chili oil is as easy to prepare as chilies pickled in vinegar. It is particularly well-suited for marinating, seasoning, and grilling and goes especially well with seafood, vegetables, and salads.

Ingredients

Makes about 1½ Cups (250 ml)

About ⅔ cup (100 g) 100 g fresh chili (each variety has a different weight!)

About 1 cup (200 g) high-grade vegetable oil

Secret Preparation

One can use any chili pepper in this recipe. One must bear in mind, however, that the color of green chili changes within twenty-four hours and becomes quite unappealing. Red, yellow, or orange chilies, on the other hand, retain their lovely color for a longer time.

First, cut the chilies into decorative rings, strips, or cubes, and then place the pieces in the bottle until half full. Then fill the bottle with oil to about ¾ inch (2 cm) below the top and place it in a dark place (i.e., a refrigerator or kitchen cupboard) for 10 days.

After this maturing period, the chili oil is ready to use and can be refined by adding garlic or herbs. The bottle should always be sealed well after use. Do not store it in the refrigerator, however, for the oil will gel and become unappealing. It is best to store it in the dark and in a place that is not too warm.

LOUISIANA-STYLE CHILI SAUCE

This sauce is normally made with fresh chilies, which are fermented. Making a true Louisiana sauce takes a great deal of work. One can, however, achieve one's goal more easily with the cooked variants.

Ingredients
Makes about 4 cups (1 liter)

2.2 pounds (1 kg) of chilies (the hotter the better)

About 2 cups (500 ml) vinegar

5 heaping tsp. salt

About 2 cups (500 ml) water

Secret Preparation

Remove the green stems from the chilies and chop finely. Place the chilies in a pot with the vinegar, salt and water; cook for 30 minutes. Remove from the pot and puree fine with an immersion blender; then cook for another 15 minutes. Add a little water if necessary. Pass the sauce through a sieve while hot and pour into bottles.

Should the sauce be too thick, you can thin it with vinegar.

ORIGINAL LOUISIANA HOT SAUCE

The original Louisiana hot sauce is made from fresh raw chilies and is not cooked. One must, therefore, proceed very carefully during preparation. The chilies are fermented, which makes preparation very time-consuming.

Ingredients

Makes about 6 to 8 cups (1½-2 liters)

2.2 pounds (1 kg) fresh chilies
About ⅓-½ cup (100 ml) water
3 ⅓ tablespoons (60 g) salt
4 tbsp. sauerkraut juice or Brottrunk (a fermented grain beverage))
About 6-8 cups (1½-2 liters) vinegar

Secret Preparation

★ ★ ★ ★ ★ ★

Remove the stems from the chilies; then clean and finely chop. Mix well with water and salt. Be careful not to get any in your eyes! Then add the sauerkraut juice or Brottrunk. The lactic acid in the juice will accelerate the start of the fermentation process. Place the now very thick puree in bottles. Caution: only fill the bottles half way at most, for after a few days the sauce will begin to foam heavily. A fermentation cap is then placed lightly on the bottles, so that gases can escape. Store the bottles at room temperature for 2 to 4 weeks. The fermentation process is complete when no more foam forms.

Now, pass it through a sieve and mix with vinegar in a 1:2 ratio. Depending on the flavor, desired consistency, and hotness, one can also add the vinegar in a 1:1 ratio or omit it altogether.

Finally, the sauce is placed in small bottles and sealed—and the Original Louisiana Hot Sauce is finished. Because of the fermentation process, the chili sauce has a long shelf life.

CARIBBEAN HABANERO SAUCE

This is my absolute favorite chili sauce. For me, it is the best way to prepare chili sauces. The basic element is always chili, but then one can give one's imagination free rein. Whether onions, bananas, or mangoes (or other fruits)—one cannot go wrong—and it always tastes good. Sauces prepared this way are easily digestible and one can always try out new variations.

Ingredients

Makes about 8 cups (2 liters)

About 2 cups (500 g) chilies

5-8 tbsp. oil

2 large onions, diced

2 cloves of garlic, peeled and cut into slices

About 8 cups (2 l) water

About 3 cups (500 g) mango, diced

Juice of 3 lemons or limes

About ¾ cup (250 ml) vinegar

4-5 tsp. salt

1 tsp. pepper

1-2 tsp. cumin

1-2 tsp. coriander

Secret Preparation

Chop the chilies, place the oil in a pot, and cook the onions and garlic in the hot oil until soft. Add water before the onions begin to brown. Add the chilies and diced mango. Stir in the lemon juice, vinegar, and spices. Cook for approximately, 30 minutes. When the chilies are soft, mix everything together finely with an immersion blender. Should the sauce be too thin, boil until the desired consistency is reached. Then pour the hot mixture into bottles and seal immediately. The sauce will last at least one year if unopened.

Our Secret Tip:

Other spices that go well include allspice, cardamom, cinnamon, fennel, ginger, and sugar.

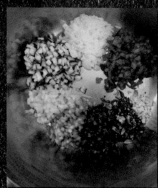

HOT CHILI SALSA
"THE MOTHER OF ALL SALSAS"

One thing first: this salsa is not for weak tongues. The heat and the flavor are staggering. The salsa is extremely versatile, is freshly prepared, and goes well with cold and quick-fried meats.

Ingredients

Makes about 10 portions

About 2¾ cup (500 g firm), fresh tomatoes or 1 can (about 3½ cups) (850-ml), peeled and diced
1 cucumber, cubed
About 1 cup (250 g) various-color chilies
1¼ cup (200 g) onion, chopped
3 tbsp (50 ml) vinegar
3 tbsp (50 ml) oil
2-3 tsp. salt
2 tbsp. sugar
2 lemons or limes
½ tsp. pepper
2-3 cloves of garlic, if desired
1 bunch garden herbs

Secret Preparation

First peel the tomatoes. If that is too time-consuming, use diced tomatoes from a can. To skin the tomatoes, first prepare a bowl large enough to hold all the tomatoes with cold water. Bring a pot of water to boiling. While waiting, remove the stems and make a crosswise cut on the opposite end. With a slotted spoon, immerse each tomato in the boiling water for 10 seconds, remove it, and immediately place it in the bowl of cold water. Treat all of the tomatoes in this way. The skins can now be removed easily. Quarter the tomatoes, cut out the interior tomato flesh, and place it in a bowl. Dice the tomato flesh into equal-sized pieces and place in a second bowl. Peel the cucumber, halve lengthwise, scrape out the soft interior with a tablespoon, and place in the bowl with the tomato insides.

Dice the chilies, the onions, and the cucumber into small pieces. Puree the tomato and cucumber insides finely. Now add vinegar, oil, salt, sugar, lemon juice, and pepper, and mix together well. Place the diced tomatoes, chilies, cucumber, and onions in the pureed stock, add finely-chopped garlic if desired. Finally, refine with chopped garden herbs.

CHILI-CHUTNEY WITH MANGO

Chili-Mango Chutney should not be absent from any grilling event. There are many variations in preparation. The version described here not only tastes good, but also has a first-class appearance. In general, chutneys go well with all kinds of meat, game, fish, and fowl, but also with cold meat, cheese, and rice dishes.

Ingredients

Makes about 5 cups (1.2 liters)
(This is equivalent to about four to five half-pint (250-ml) preserving jars

About 2 cups (500 g) chilies
2/3 cup (150 ml vinegar))
About 1 cup (200 ml) water
1¼ cup (200 g) onion, finely chopped
1½ cups (250 g) mango, diced
2½ cups (500 g) sugar
2 tbsp. ginger
½ tsp. coriander
½ tsp. cumin
½ tsp. cinnamon
½ tsp. fenugreek
½ tsp. cardamom

Secret Preparation

★ ★ ★ ★ ☆ ☆

Chop the chilies finely. Combine vinegar with water and bring to a boil. Add the onions and chilies, cover and boil gently for 15 to 25 minutes. Add the mango, the sugar, and the spices; mix well and then boil for 10 to 20 minutes.

When the consistency is similar to that of marmalade, place in jars and seal well.

The chutney can last for approximately one to three weeks in the refrigerator. Apples, bananas, pears, or peaches can be used instead of mango.

CHILI JAM

Chili jam is extremely popular as a dip for grilled chicken pieces, but should not be confused with the mild Asian sweet and hot chili sauces. Depending on the chilies used, it is extremely hot and flavorful. Chili jam can, of course, also be used to spice other dishes. (I like it very much for seasoning rice dishes.)

Ingredients

Makes about 8 cups (2 liters)

(This is equivalent to about eight half-pint (250-ml) preserving jars)
About 4 cups (1 kg) chilies
About ½ cup (100 ml) water (really 27/64 cups)
About ½ cup (100 ml) lemon juice
5 cups(1 kg) preserving sugar

Secret Preparation

Wash the chili peppers, remove the green stems, halve them, and remove the cores. Then cut into fine cubes or process medium-fine in a blender or food processer.

Place the processed chili in a pot and mix with water, lemon juice and preserving sugar. Boil for 30 minutes, stirring constantly. Pour into jam jars while still hot and seal immediately. If the jam is poured into the jars in layers, the chili pieces will remain suspended.

CULINARY TIPS FOR USING CHILI

Mix some **medium-hot mustard** with chili sauce and you have hot mustard.

Chili gives sour pickled vegetables the right pep.

Pickles become hot if combined with chili pepper.

Olives become fiery if chili sauce or chili peppers are added to the bottle.

Yogurt with 1 tbsp. honey and ½ tsp. Caribbean Habanero Sauce—delicious.

For colds, **difficulty sleeping, and cold feet,** a glass of warm milk with 2 tbsp. honey and ½ tsp. homemade chili sauce (or Hot Mamas Chili Sauce) helps.

Jam tastes especially good with a splash of homemade chili sauce.

Cherry liqueur or crème cassis can be enriched by adding a shot of chili sauce.

Adding a chili pepper during cooking produces a finely spiced rice.

Fresh cheese mixed with chili gives the right kick.

A shot of chili makes even the most boring canned stew a memorable experience.

Make an exotic cup of hot chocolate by adding ½ tsp. Caribbean Habanero Chili Sauce.

Cook potatoes in red beet juice with one or two chili peppers to make red chili potatoes.

Chocolate pudding with raspberry sauce and several drops of Caribbean Habanero Chili Sauce tastes great.

Vanilla ice cream with strawberries and several drops of Caribbean Habanero Chili Sauce still tastes like ice cream, but hot.

A simple noodle soup becomes an Oriental soup by adding a teaspoon of chili sauce.

Ketchup becomes fiery when it is spiced with chili sauce.

FAMILIAR CHILI SAUCES & SMALL MANUFACTURERS

USA

TABASCO
McIlhenny/Avery Island, Louisiana

The McIlhenny Family business has produced the famous Tabasco Sauce since 1868, and it is the undisputed world brand leader. Tabasco is exported to 164 countries.

In addition to the big manufacturers, there is a local sauce maker in almost every American city. These are small manufacturers, who elevate their sauces above the broad masses by constantly changing their formulas and giving them unusual names.

Here are the most well-known:

CAJOHNS
Columbus, Ohio

The founder of Cajohns — John Hard — is my greatest inspiration and a personal friend. John has been producing sauces since 1996. He has become famous in Europe for sauces like Black Mamba and Vicious Viper. It is noteworthy that these sauces originated from Harald Zoschke, who had a sauce company in the USA. He sold his business in the USA to Cajohn and returned to Germany. There he opened Pepperwood, a hot sauce shop. He ran the shop very successfully for years and he authored *The Chili Pepper Book*. He has since sold his business and now devotes his time exclusively to writing. In Germany he is an eminent authority in chili matters.

DAVE'S GOURMET
San Francisco, California, owner Dave Hirschkop

The inventor of the Ultra Hot Sauces, Dave was the first to use chili extract in his sauces. He was expelled from the Fiery Food Show in New Mexico after numerous complaints—as the sauce was hotter than anything previously tasted. The press picked up the story and as a result he became quasi-famous overnight. Everyone wanted his product, which became world famous under the name Dave's Insanity Sauce.

BLAIR'S Long Branch, New Jersey

Since 1989, Blair Lazar has been producing his ultra-hot Death and Mega-Death sauces. He is a prehistoric rock in the hot sauce scene.

GERMANY

HOT MAMAS Pforzheim, Baden-Wurttemberg

Germany's first hot sauce maker has been around since 2006. Hot Mamas sauces are only available in the typical pocket flask bottles. The company makes the hottest marketable sauce in Europe. It bears the name Painmaker Hardcore. In order to be able to take part in the Fiery Food Show, I established the Chili Police Spicy Food Company in the USA. There I introduced the German sauce with the name Painmaker Hardcore. It is so hot that paramedics soon had to administer first-aid to several hyperventilating people. For this reason, the show wanted to ban our German team from further participation, but in the end we were allowed to stay—though under observation. The local television station reported what had happened and, the next day, countless news teams showed up. As a result of this media response, the show was literally overrun by thousands of visitors, and people stood in line for hours for a chance to try the sauce. The expression "pain train" was born. During a subsequent tour across the USA, I discovered one of the oldest BBQ sauce recipes in a small Texas town on Route 66. Almost all of the grill and BBQ sauces made by my company are based on this recipe.

TRADE FAIRS & EVENTS

FIERY FOOD SHOW
Albuquerque, New Mexico

Under the patronage of Dave de Witt, the Pope of Chilies, the national Fiery Foods and BBQ Show has been held in Albuquerque, New Mexico, for twenty-six years. Since then this trade show for hot foods has become the most important platform for makers of hot sauces from around the world.

The show is held annually at the beginning of March. Dave de Witt has written countless books about chili peppers and is the worldwide eminent authority in chili matters. Anyone who wants to experience the crazy world of hot sauce makers for himself simply has to go.

ZEST FEST
Irving, Texas

In Texas, the last weekend in January is completely under the shadow of spicy heat. Anyone in the area or on vacation in Texas at that time should definitely drop in. While the fest is not as well-known as the Fiery Food Show in Albuquerque, one will definitely find the same exhibitors there.

CAJUN HOT SAUCE FESTIVAL
Sugarena At Acadiana Fairgrounds, New Iberia, Los Angeles

Fifteen thousand people come for a weekend to take in cook-offs, hot food-eating contests, and much more.

NEW YORK CITY HOT SAUCE EXPO

East River State Park, 110 Kent Ave, Brooklyn, New York

Small but good. It is always held in April, with live music, plenty of alcohol, eating competitions, BBQ, and much more. If in New York, one should definitely set aside half a day to go see the craziness.

MIDWEST WING FEST

St. Claire Square Mall, Fairview Heights, Illinois

At the end of August, up to 40,000 visitors storm the mall and eat chicken wings of every kind. It is difficult to imagine the quantity of chicken wings that is consumed. A varied supporting program delights the audience.

SECRET TIPS

Ohio, USA

The North Market Fiery Foods Festival in Columbus, Ohio, takes place in mid-February. There is a wide variety of events in a cozy atmosphere, from cooking demonstrations to barbecue contests and hot food-eating competitions.

Jungle Jim's Weekend of Fire takes place in Cincinnati, Ohio, at the beginning of October. Jungle Jim's is a supermarket of the superlative. It looks like a zoo, with life-sized plastic animals, a real fishing boat in the fish department, and a real fire truck where the shelves for hot sauces are located. Unique in all the world. All of the important hot sauce makers in the US meet here. Much show and conversation. You have to see it.

At Cajohns, 816 Green Crest Drive, Westerville/Columbus, Ohio, one can simply drop in and meet the legends all year round. There is plenty to see and one quickly becomes involved in conversation. Ask for John or Sue and convey greetings from me (Painmaker and the Chili Police) and you will be warmly welcomed.

BLOGGERS

Al Buddah Goldenberg (ILoveitSpicy.com)

I have known Al the longest; he provides plenty of background information and is always up to date. Serious, funny, and honest. There is probably no one from the sauce scene that he does not know.

Scott Roberts (ScottRobertsWeb.com) is well-organized and his information is helpful.

Ted Barrus, the Fire Breathing Idiot (tedbarrus on Youtube) is a crazy fellow, ruthless and open. His postings are worth seeing. It is incredible how much pain he can endure. In any case, he is always informed about the latest sauces and their effects.

... AND FOR ALL THOSE WHO DON'T LIKE IT QUITE AS HOT, WE NOW CONTINUE WITH GRILL AND BARBECUE SAUCES...

GRILLING IS A MAN'S JOB

Sometime during a long working day a million years ago, so the legend goes, *Homo rudolfensis* discovered fire and thus began the first barbecue in human history— for the mammoth he had killed had to be cooked somehow, and this was done squatting on the ground beside a Stone Age grill.

Since then women have evolved, and they now cook with computer-controlled induction stoves, micro-wave ovens, and low-temperature ovens.

It would thus appear that the evolution of the man was reduced to moving the campfire to a metal bowl standing on three legs, and this only because man had by then gone upright and found stooping difficult.

Why then should the woman feel disadvantaged?

Every woman wants a strong man at her side. She would like him to be the monarch, master and macho for one day of the week, because during the remaining six days she looks after her man, controls his destiny, manages his money, and decides which hobbies are good for him.

I would go so far as to contend that grilling was invented by wom-en, in order to allow the man to go on believing that he is master of the house. Because, as everyone knows, the way to a man's heart is through his stomach, one cannot know too much about the secrets of preparing sauces.

THE MEANING OF THE WORD: BBQ/BARBECUE

The word has its origins in the Mexican-Spanish term *barbacoa*, which is derived from the Taino word *buccan*. This had previously referred to the wooden frame on which the Taino people prepared meat over an open fire. The first written mention of *barbacoa* is found in Gonzalo Fernández de Oviedo's *De la historia General y Natural de las Indias* written in 1526.

At the time of the Spanish conquest of the Americas, the preparation method of cooking meat slowly in smoke was common throughout the entire Caribbean and along the coast of the mainland as far south as Brazil. Bernal Díaz del Castillo, whose book *The True History of the Conquest of New Spain* gave an eyewitness account of the Spanish conquest from 1519 to 1521 and knew about *barbacoa*. However, Díaz del Castillo used the term in reference to meat that was roasted in pits in what is now Mexico.

The fact that the words for the pirates of the Caribbean in Spanish, French, and English (*bucanero, boucanier,* and *buccaneer*) are also derived from the Taino word *buccan* is further evidence of the close association with the Caribbean. Similar preparation methods, or jerk, have survived in Central America and the Caribbean. In Mexico, whole goats were cooked over a fire at low temperatures, while in Cuba a pig smoked in a pit is considered a traditional Christmas meal.

The Spanish played their part in the creation of modern barbecuing by introducing the pig and thus pork to the New World. The word "barbecue" first appeared in the *Oxford English Dictionary* in 1661, but it only referred to the wooden frame. A few decades later, it referred exclusively to the meal; in 1733, for example, Benjamin Lynde, magistrate of the Province of Massachusetts, mentioned barbecue in his writings, as did George Washington and Thomas Jefferson later.

Even though the first mention of barbecue originated from Virginia, in the long run, no strong barbecue tradition was able to establish itself there. The Carolinas (North and South) are regarded as the "cradle of the barbecue," and there are even major local differences in the manner of preparation there. Like many dishes from the southern states, barbecue was also influenced by African-American cuisine. Many cooks were slaves who had come to the southern states from the Caribbean, where they had become familiar with Caribbean cooking and spices.

Before explaining the difference between grill and barbecue sauces and starting into the recipes, I will delve into ketchup, as a sort of individual and universal genius.

... AND THAT IS ALL FOUND IN A GOOD HOMEMADE KETCHUP.

KETCHUP

Ketchup is a jack-of-all-trades and, at the same time, the simplest grill sauce of all. A world without ketchup is simply inconceivable. There are thousands of different recipes and taste variations. Ketchup has been with us since our childhood, and it simply goes with everything. Here is a great basic recipe that you can modify with other spices and additives to suit your taste.

Ingredients

Makes approximately 4 cups (1 liter)

35 ounces (1.2 kg) of peeled tomatoes from the can (or fresh fleshy tomatoes)
tsp. ground pepper
2 tsp. ground ginger
1 clove of garlic or ½ tsp. garlic powder
1 large onion, finely chopped or 1 tsp. onion powder
2 tsp. salt
5 tbsp. sugar
½ tsp. coriander
½ tsp. fenugreek
1 tsp. cumin
3 tbsp. (50 ml) vinegar

Secret Preparation

If you would like to use fresh tomatoes, they must first be peeled. Make a crosswise cut on one side, submerge them in boiling water for 10 seconds and then immediately place them in cold water. The skin can then be removed easily. Chop the tomatoes finely and place them in a pot with the other ingredients. Cook over low to medium heat for 30 minutes, stirring occasionally, then puree with an immersion blender. If necessary, continue cooking until the desired consistency is achieved. It should be a smooth ketchup. The ketchup will become thicker when cooled.

If desired, the recipe can be modified by adding the following ingredients:

Chili, curry, ginger, honey, plums, peppercorns or cinnamon.

USING BARBECUE & GRILL SAUCES
(BBQ SAUCES)

BBQ sauces:

These come in many flavors and, because of their smoky taste, which varies from "sweet" to "sweet-hot" to "very hot" and "very sour," are primarily used for marinating. During cooking they are used for mopping, and they are also used to add flavor to pulled meats (such as pulled pork).

Marinating:

The purpose of marinating is to allow the spices to penetrate deep into the meat. Marinating also makes the meat more tender. It is rubbed with or immersed in the BBQ sauce and left in the refrigerator for 12-24 hours to marinate. The marinade is then discarded.

Mopping:

Mopping is the process during grilling in which one applies BBQ sauce with a small mop or brush. Mopping results in a higher concentration of spices on the meat. The sauce caramelizes over the coals, creating a pleasing color and a crisp crust.

Spicing:

After it is "pulled," pulled pork is spiced with BBQ sauce. The preferred sauce is poured over the meat and everything is mixed together.

Important: BBQ sauces always have a powerful, smoky aroma and enhance the desired smoke flavor of the meat.

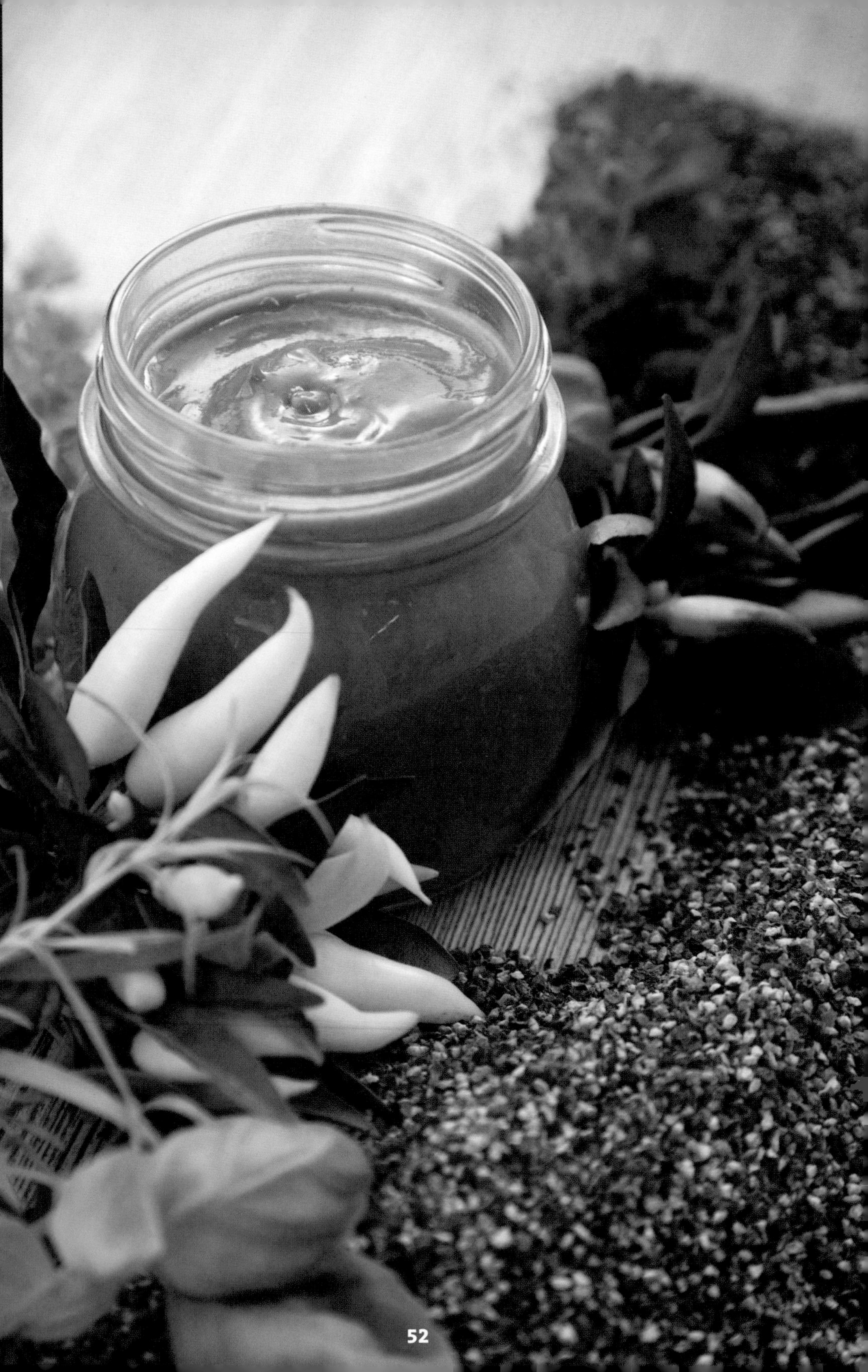

GRILL SAUCES
(STEAK SAUCES)

Steak sauce, grill sauce, or gourmet sauce:
three names for the same sauce.
They are eaten with grilled foods.

As a sauce:

Pour the sauce directly from the
bottle onto the plate or steak.

As a dip:

Place the sauce separately in a bowl,
into which the grilled meat is dipped.

For coating:

On chicken wings, for example. The wings are placed
in a bowl; then a hot grill sauce is added and the
chicken wings are turned until coated.

Steak sauce, grill sauce, or gourmet sauce does not
have a smoky aroma. Instead, it is rather hot, sweet,
sweet-hot, and often quite sour. Grill sauces are
eaten with meat rather casually. They should suit
the taste of the consumer, create the desire for more,
and never abet the overdosing of smoke aromas.

If we compare BBQ and grill sauces, the only obvious
difference is the presence or absence of smoke flavor.

Secret Tip:
A BBQ sauce without smoke is a grill sauce, and a grill sauce with
smoke flavor is a BBQ sauce.

STEAK SAUCE, GRILL SAUCE...

THE TRUE HISTORY OF THE ORIGINS OF BBQ SAUCE

There are a thousand and one stories about the BBQ sauce legend, but I will tell the true one. To understand the story, one must be aware of the following: to preserve food, it was usually pickled or bottled. Tomatoes were picked while still half green to prevent spoilage. As a result, preserved tomatoes were a rather "bitter-sour" affair. We are speaking of the year 1849 when the Gold Rush was in full swing. Streams of settlers were heading for the gold fields, accompanied by countless Chinese coolies. The Chinese built railroads, worked in the mines, and served as cooks. A Chinese cook was supposed to use the supplies at hand to prepare a tasty dish.

Meat was roasted over an open fire and there were baked beans, which were mixed with preserved tomatoes. The bitter-sour tomatoes were not exactly a culinary highlight. The ambitious Chinese cooks knew how to help themselves and combined Worcestershire Sauce from England, *ketjap* (Chinese soy sauce), plenty of molasses, several Asian spices, and dried chili to enhance the flavor. The sour-bitter taste was thus eliminated and the result overwhelming. The gold seekers liked the dish so much that they used the ingredients intended for baked beans to make a sauce. This sauce was an outstanding condiment that went well with any dish, whether vegetables or meat. The BBQ sauce was born. The modern term "ketchup" also probably comes from the Asian word "ketjap." The sauce was first made commercially in the U.S. by Henry John Heinz, who was descended from German immigrants. Today, Heinz is the worldwide market leader in ketchup.

Over the years there have been endless variations in BBQ sauces, although one can easily verify whether there has in fact been an improvement in taste: since 2013, there has been a sauce made using the original recipe of 1849.

It is called Painmaker BBQ Sauce—Old School—US Style—1849. What sets it apart are the selected ingredients, which are the same as those used in 1849 and thus guarantee a unique taste experience.

RECIPES

The degree of
difficulty in
preparation is
indicated by ★

★ ☆ ☆ ☆ ☆ ☆

very easy

★ ★ ★ ★ ★ ★

very difficult

ORIGINAL TEXAS BBQ SAUCE

An original Texan BBQ sauce made from the basic ketchup recipe. Every barbecue sauce uses ketchup as its base.

Ingredients

Makes about 4 cups (1 liter)

About 28 ounces (800 g) ketchup (homemade or purchased)
2 level tsp. salt
12 tbsp. soy sauce
12 tbsp. Worcestershire Sauce
8-10 tbsp. sugar beet molasses
2 tsp. pepper, coarse ground
1 clove of garlic or 1 tsp. garlic powder
1 small onion, finely diced or 1 tsp. onion powder
1-2 tsp. chipotle powder (or any other chili)
1.2 tsp pepper
1 tsp cumin
1-2 tbsp. liquid smoke

Secret Preparation

Place the ketchup in a pot with the other ingredients. Let cook at low to medium heat for 10-15 minutes, stirring occasionally. Puree the sauce with an immersion blender. If necessary, boil further to achieve the desired consistency. It should be a rather thick sauce. It will become firmer when it cools. The taste can be varied endlessly by adding whisky, red wine, pepper, or chili.

ORIGINAL STEAK SAUCE

Steak sauce is often called grill sauce or gourmet sauce. Using the basic ketchup recipe to create an original steak sauce is quite easy. Ketchup is also always the basis for steak sauce.

Ingredients

Makes about 4 cups (1 liter)

About 28 ounces (800 g) ketchup (homemade or purchased)
2 level tsp. salt
12 tbsp. soy sauce
12 tbsp. Worchester Sauce
8-10 tbsp. sugar beet molasses
2 tsp. pepper, coarse ground
1 clove of garlic or 1 tsp. garlic powder
1 small onion, finely diced or 1 tsp. onion powder
1-2 tsp. chipotle powder (or any other chili)
1.2 tsp pepper
1 tsp cumin

Secret Preparation

Place all of the ingredients in a pot. Let cook at low to medium heat for 20-30 minutes, stirring occasionally. Puree the steak sauce with an immersion blender. If necessary, boil further to achieve the desired consistency. The sauce should be a rather viscous. Bottle while still warm and seal well. The sauce will become firmer when it cools.

The taste can be varied by adding whisky, pepper, or chili.

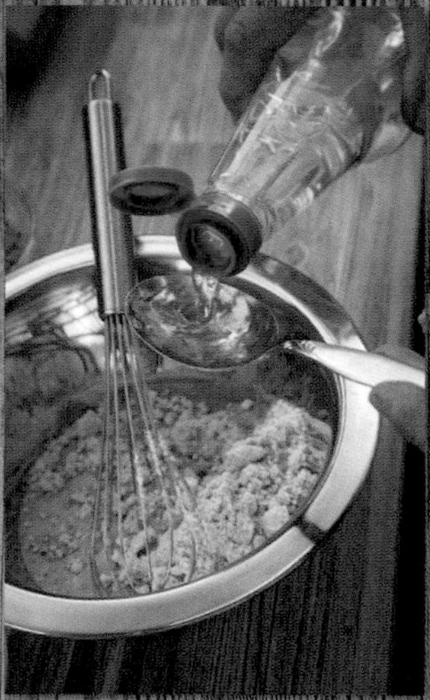

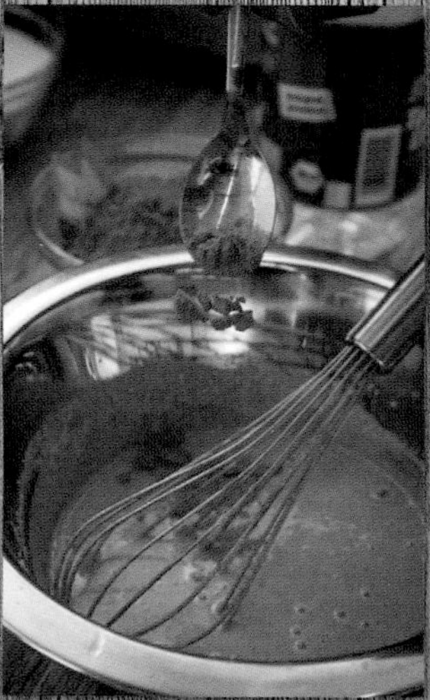

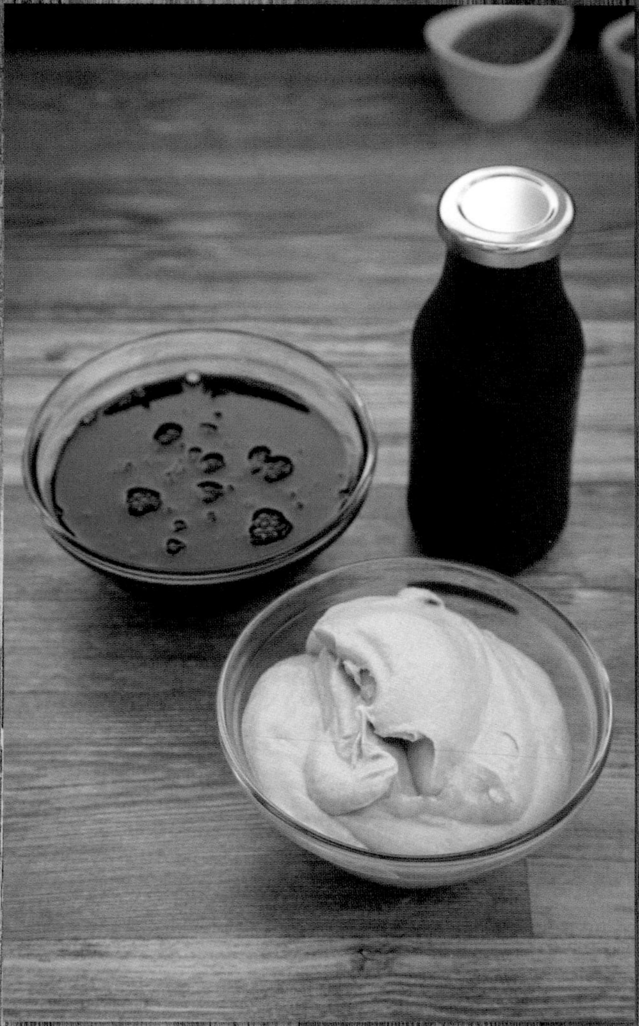

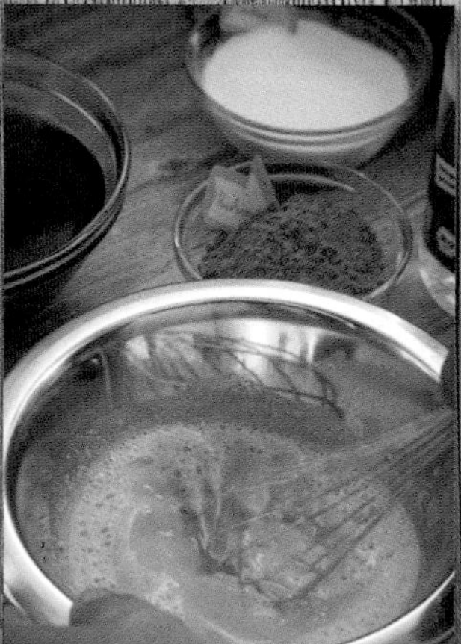

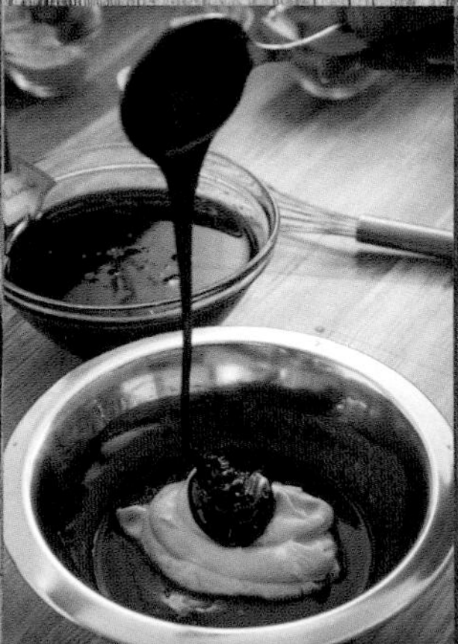

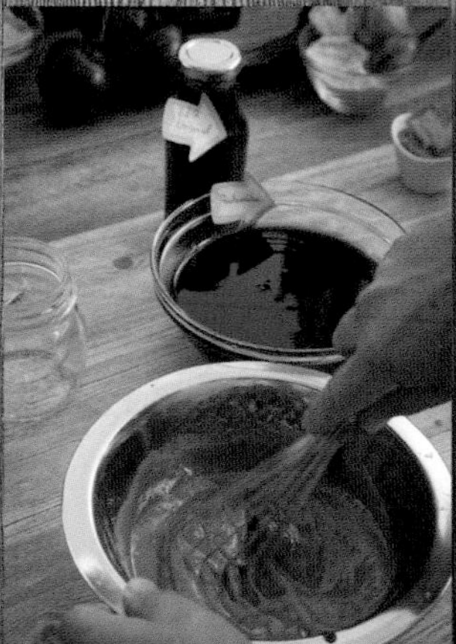

BBQ-MUSTARD SAUCE

This BBQ mustard sauce is something quite special. The recipe comes from the Carolinas, where it is used at almost every barbecue. Try it with Weisswurst (sausage), with salmon, and as a salad dressing, although it will need to be thinned for the latter.

Mustard is easy to make at home—here is a quick recipe:

Ingredients

Makes about 28 ounces
(200 g) of mustard

6 heaping tbsp. ground mustard (not de-oiled)
6 tbsp. vinegar
1 tsp. salt
2 tsp. sugar
½ tsp. turmeric
6 tbsp. water

Secret Preparation

Combine all ingredients in a bowl with 6 tbsp. of water and mix together well.

Ingredients

Makes about 8 ounces (250 g) sauce

8 heaping tbsp. mustard
7 tbsp. BBQ sauce
2 tbsp. sugar beet molasses

Secret Preparation

Mix all ingredients together well in a bowl. The color should be ochre-yellow. The flavor can be varied by adding whisky, cognac, pepper, or chili.

HONEY-MUSTARD SAUCE

Honey-mustard sauce works extremely well for marinating, as mustard is a natural tenderizer. Try it with Weisswurst, salmon or, thinned somewhat, as a salad dressing.

Ingredients

Makes 8 ounces (250 g) sauce

6 heaping tbsp. mustard (not de-oiled)
6 tbsp. vinegar
6 tbsp. water
1 tsp. salt
2 tsp. sugar
½ tsp. turmeric
4-5 tbsp. honey, to your taste

Secret Preparation

Combine all ingredients in a bowl and mix together well. The sauce should have a bright yellow color. It will thicken more in the bottle.

The flavor can be varied by adding whiskey, cognac, pepper, ginger, chili, tarragon, and chervil or dill.

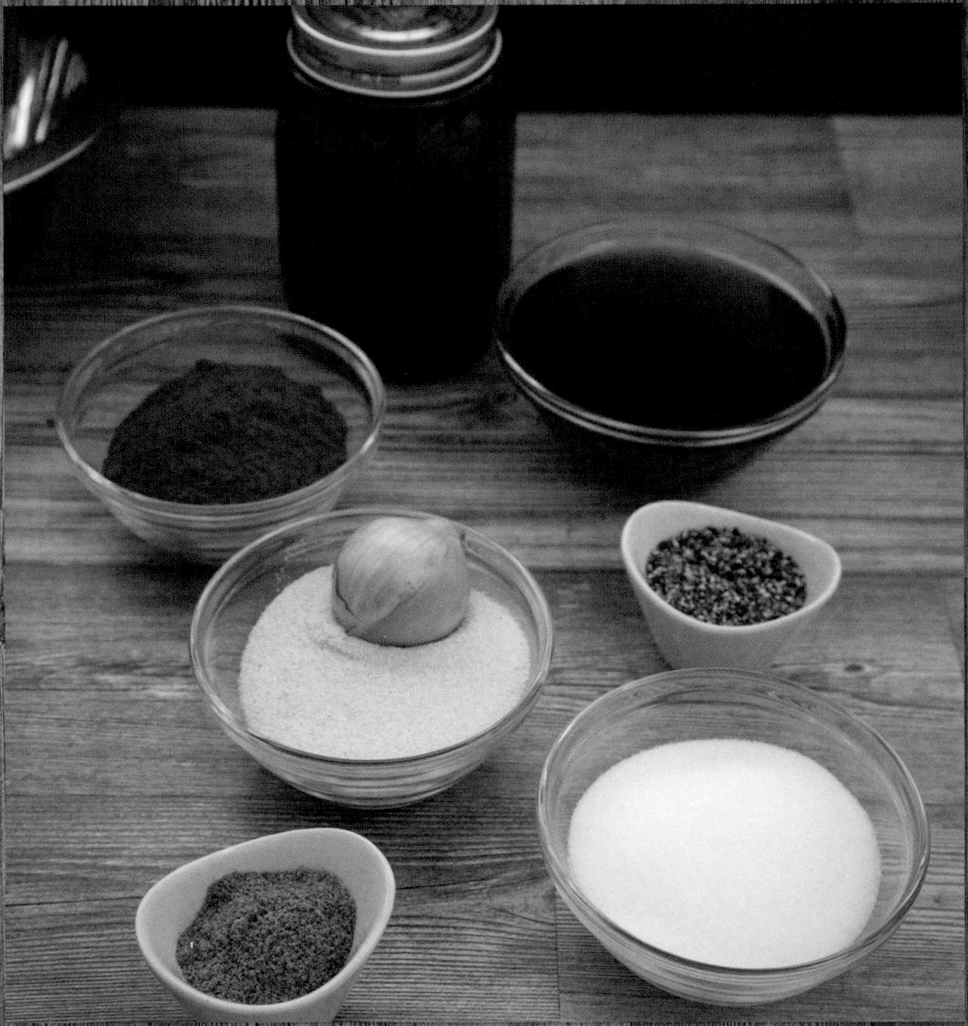

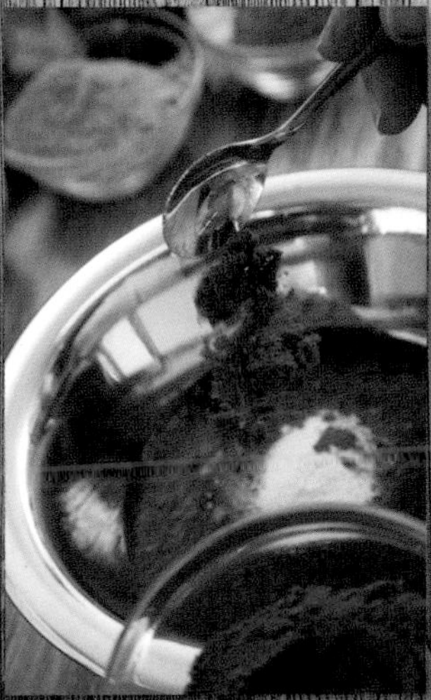

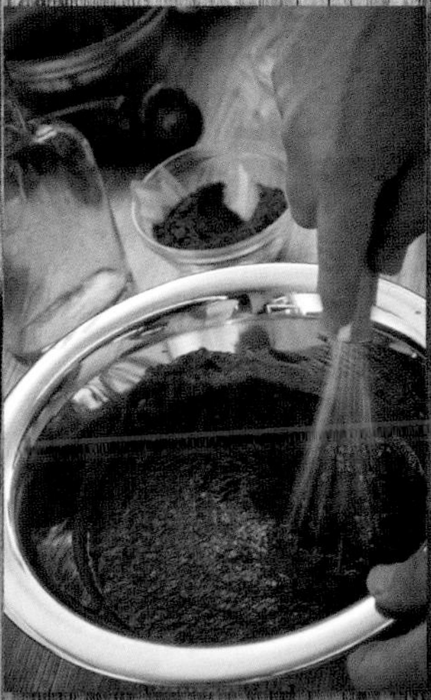

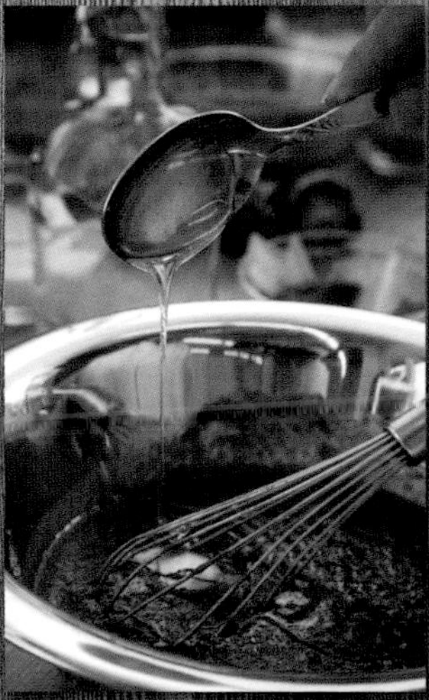

CHICKEN WING SAUCE

A barbecue isn't a barbecue without chicken wings and the appropriate sauce. A chicken wing sauce should be as sweet as love and as sharp as a razor blade. It should taste so good that one doesn't want to stop eating. The tears in the corners of the eyes will then probably be tears of joy.

Ketchup is the basis of the sauce. Thus we can make an original chicken wing sauce from the basic ketchup recipe:

Ingredients

Makes 8 ounces (250 g)

About 7 ounces (200 g) ketchup (homemade or store-bought)
¼ tsp. coriander
½ tbsp. cumin
1 tsp. ginger
1 tsp. ground pepper
1 tsp. salt
1 tsp. onion powder
2-4 tsp. chili powder (a hot variety if possible, such as Habanero)
2-3 tsp. honey

Secret Preparation

Mix all the ingredients together well. The chicken wing sauce is well-suited for dipping or coating the wings. Simply cover the wings well with sauce before putting in the oven.

One can also vary the flavor of this recipe by adding whisky, beer, cognac, or ginger.

MAYONNAISE

Mayonnaise

Remoulade

Tomato Whiskey

Lime

SAUCES

Tartar Sauce

Chipotle Chili

Curry-Ginger

Pepper

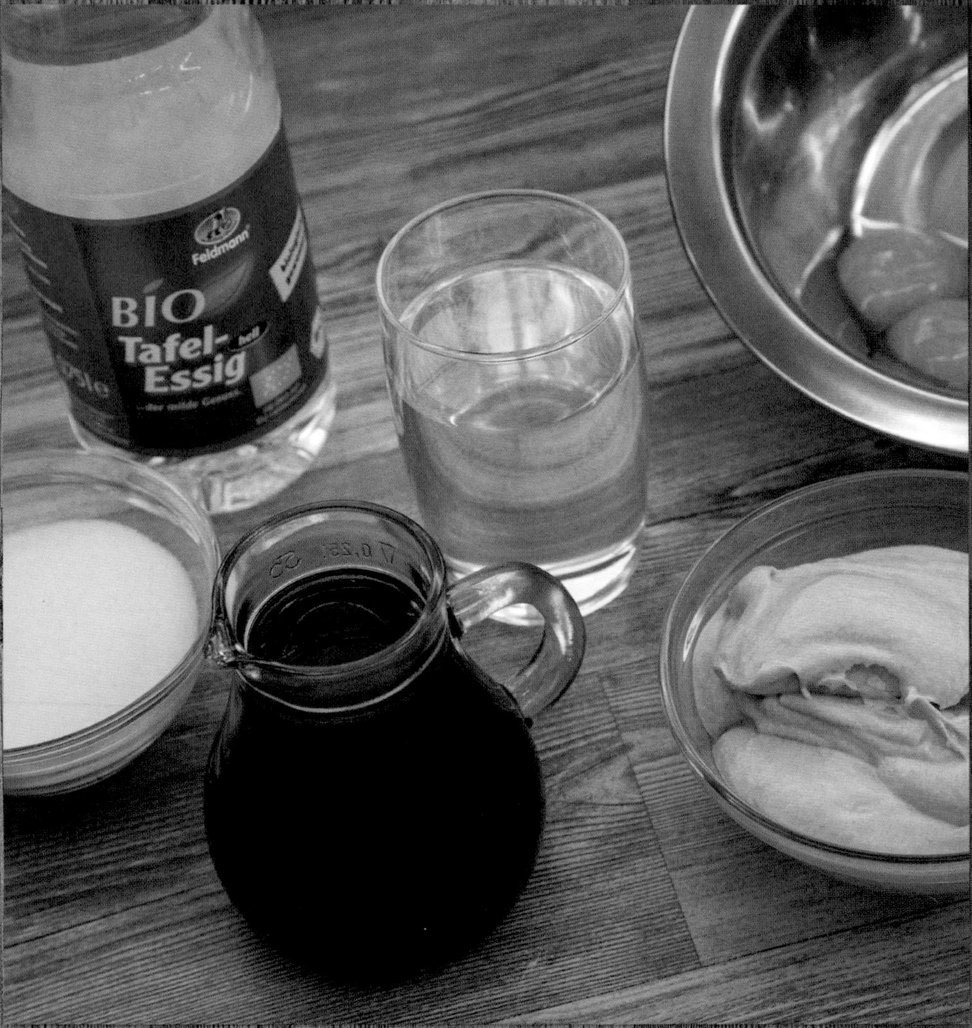
Feldmann
BIO
Tafel-
Essig

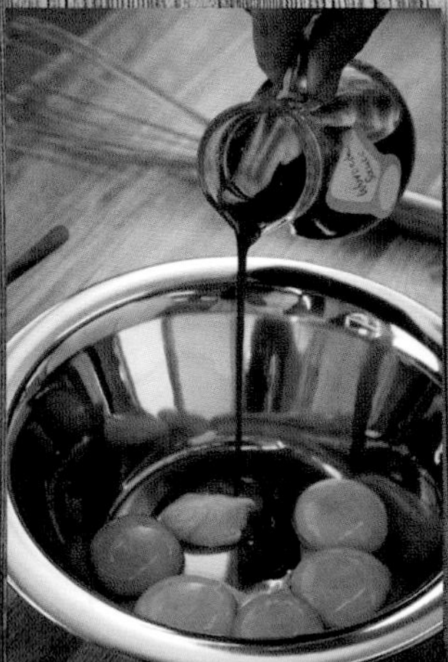

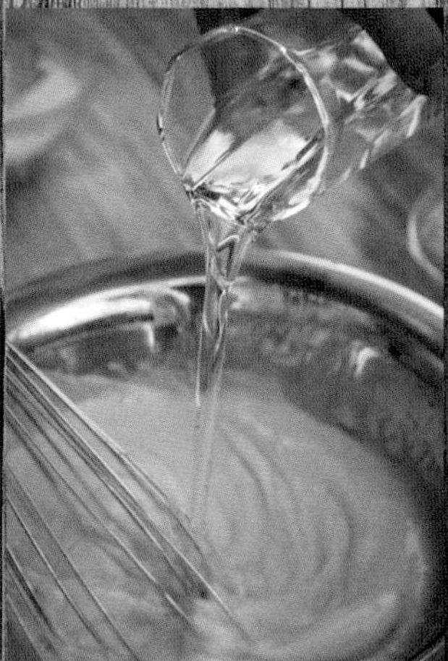

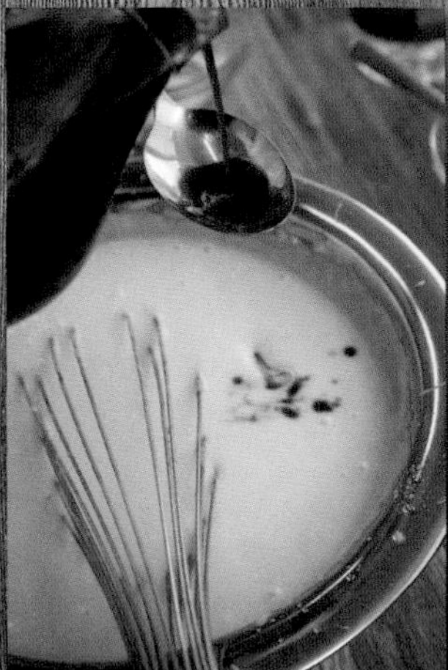

MAYONNAISE

Is mayonnaise a barbecue sauce? But of course! In Alabama, "BBQ White" is a traditional part of barbecuing. The basic ingredient is always mayonnaise, which can be modified by adding new ingredients.

Based on a mayonnaise recipe tested a thousand times, which can be prepared quickly and confidently, I reveal to you the best recipes from Alabama. (These sauces are enjoyed with fondue in Germany.)

Ingredients

Makes 1½ cups (300 g)

2 egg yolks
2 tsp. mustard
¼-½ tsp Worcester Sauce
1 pinch of salt
¼ tsp. sugar
1 pinch white pepper
About 1 cup (250 g) oil
2 tsp. vinegar

Secret Preparation

To succeed in preparing this recipe, the oil and egg yolks should be at room temperature.

Combine all of the ingredients, except the oil, in a not-too-large bowl and mix well. This is best done with an immersion blender or hand mixer, but a regular whisk will also do the job. My favorite is the immersion blender.

Stir the mixture while slowly but surely adding the oil. If the oil combines with the egg yolks, then all is going well. If not, add the oil more slowly.

If the mixture is too thick, then simply mix in some water. By adding some vinegar at the end, the mayonnaise will become somewhat thicker and also lighter in color.

ALABAMA HOT MAYONNAISE

Alabama Hot Mayonnaise can of course be eaten with any fondue dish, especially one that you would like to be a little hotter.

Ingredients

Makes 1½ cups (300 g)

2 egg yolks
2 tsp. mustard
¼-½ tsp. Worcester Sauce
2 tsp. vinegar
1 pinch of salt
¼ tsp. sugar
1 pinch white pepper
About 1 cup (250 g) oil
2-6 tsp. cayenne pepper, according to taste

Secret Preparation

To succeed in preparing this recipe, the oil and egg yolks should be at room temperature.

Combine all of the ingredients, except the oil and cayenne pepper, in a not-too-large bowl and mix well.

This is best done with an immersion blender or hand mixer, but a regular whisk will also do the job. My favorite is the immersion blender.

Stir the mixture, while slowly but surely adding the oil. If the oil combines with the egg yolks, then all is going well. If not, add the oil more slowly.

If the mixture is too thick, then simply mix in some water. By adding some vinegar at the end, the mayonnaise will become somewhat thicker and also lighter in color. Add the cayenne pepper at the very end.

Note: Now is the time to precisely determine the degree of hotness.

ALABAMA CURRY-GINGER MAYONNAISE

This version goes well with poultry and vegetables—for everyone who likes it exotic . . .

Ingredients

Makes 1½ cups (300 g)

2 egg yolks
2 tsp. mustard
¼-½ tsp Worcester Sauce
2 tsp. vinegar
1 pinch of salt
¼ tsp. sugar
1 pinch white pepper
About 1 cup (250 g) oil
2-4 tsp. curry powder, according to taste
2 tsp. fresh ginger, chopped very fine
2-3 tbsp. honey

Secret Preparation

To succeed in preparing this recipe, the oil and egg yolks should be at room temperature.

Combine all of the ingredients, except the oil, curry, ginger, and honey, in a not-too-large bowl and mix well. This is best done with an immersion blender or hand mixer, but a regular whisk will also do the job. My favorite is the immersion blender.

Stir the mixture while slowly but surely adding the oil. If the oil combines with the egg yolks, then all is going well. If not, add the oil more slowly.

If the mixture is too thick, then simply mix in some water. By adding some vinegar at the end, the mayonnaise will become somewhat thicker and also lighter in color. Mix in the curry, ginger, and honey at the very end.

Note: The ginger makes the mayonnaise hot!

ALABAMA LIME MAYONNAISE

This mayonnaise goes very well with fish (including smoked fish), poultry, and roast beef. It is exactly the thing for everyone who wants a sour freshness kick.

Ingredients

Makes 1½ cups (300 g)

2 egg yolks
2 tsp. mustard
¼-½ tsp Worcester Sauce
2 tsp. vinegar
1 pinch of salt
¼ tsp. sugar
1 pinch white pepper
About 1 cup (250 g) oil
Juice of 4 limes

Secret Preparation

To succeed in preparing this recipe, the oil and egg yolks should be at room temperature.

Combine all of the ingredients except the oil in a not-too-large bowl and mix well. This is best done with an immersion blender or hand mixer, but a regular whisk will also do the job. My favorite is the immersion blender.

Stir the mixture while slowly but surely adding the oil. If the oil combines with the egg yolks, then all is going well. If not, add the oil more slowly.

If the mixture is too thick, then simply mix in some water. By adding some vinegar at the end, the mayonnaise will become somewhat thicker and also lighter in color.

ALABAMA BLACK CRUSHED PEPPER MAYONNAISE

This version goes well with poultry and vegetables—for everyone who likes it exotic.

Ingredients

Makes 1½ cups (300 g)

2 egg yolks
2 tsp. mustard
¼-½ tsp Worcester Sauce
2 tsp. vinegar
1 pinch of salt
¼ tsp. sugar
About 1 cup (250 g) oil
4 tbsp. ground black pepper

Secret Preparation

To succeed in preparing this recipe, the oil and egg yolks should be at room temperature.

Combine all of the ingredients, except the oil and ground pepper, in a not-too-large bowl and mix well. This is best done with an immersion blender or hand mixer, but a regular whisk will also do the job. My favorite is the immersion blender.

Stir the mixture while slowly but surely adding the oil. If the oil combines with the egg yolks, then all is going well. If not, add the oil more slowly.

If the mixture is too thick, then simply mix in some water. By adding some vinegar at the end, the mayonnaise will become somewhat thicker and also lighter in color. Do not add the ground pepper until the very end.

Secret Tip:

I recommend the best pepper in the world: Tasmanian Mountain Pepper. It is, however, also the most expensive pepper in the world.

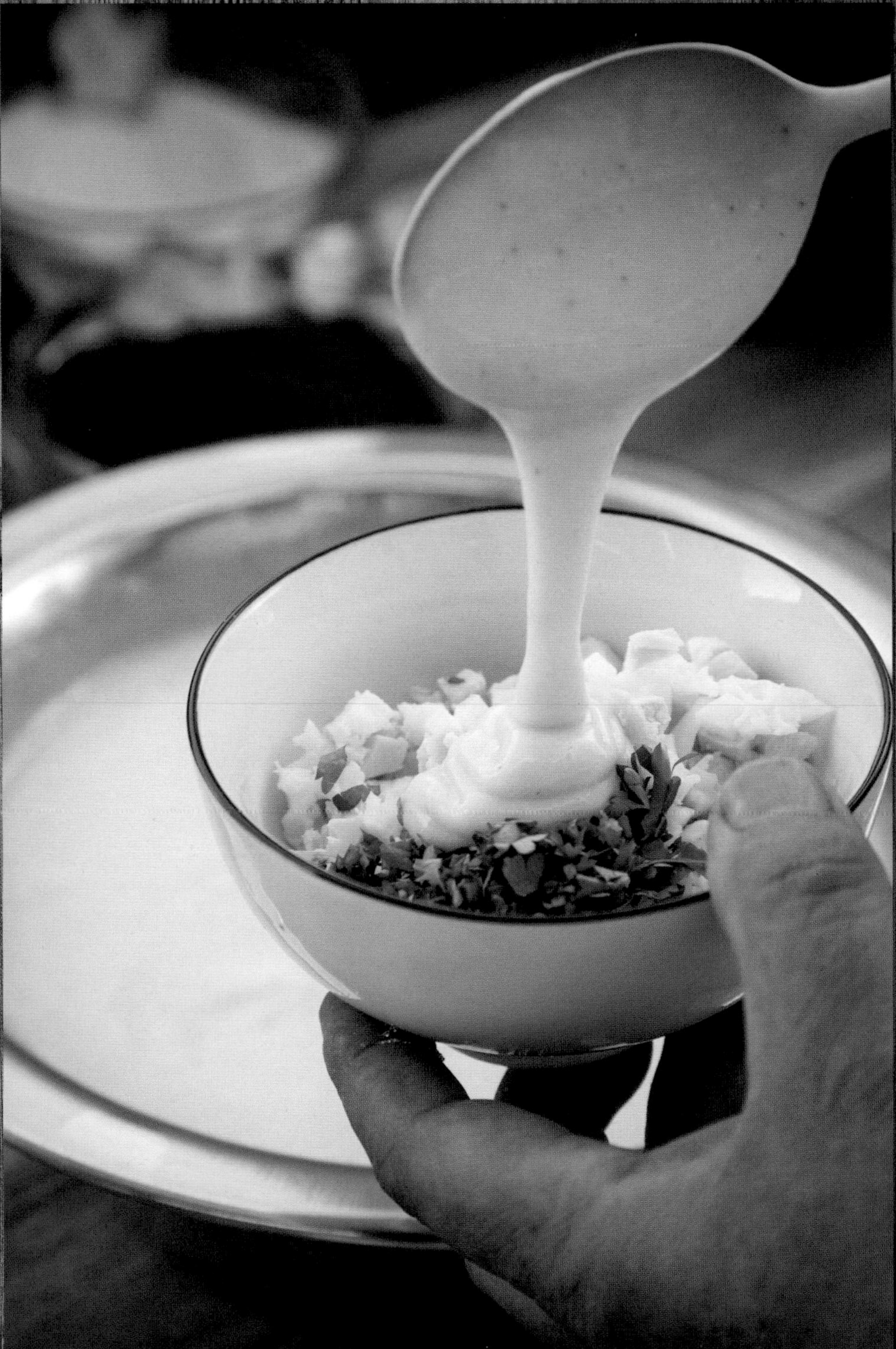

ALABAMA EGG & HERB MAYONNAISE

Goes best with roast beef, all kinds of cold, cooked meats, potato salad, roasted fish, and fried chicken.

The Alabama Egg and Herb Mayonnaise is a derivative of remoulade, but without the anchovies, capers, and gherkins.

Ingredients

Makes 1½ cups (300 g)

2 egg yolks
2 tsp. mustard
¼-½ tsp Worcester Sauce
2 tsp. vinegar
1 pinch of salt
¼ tsp. sugar
About 1 cup (250 g) oil
3 hardboiled eggs
4 tbsp. kitchen herbs (parsley, tarragon, and chervil)

Secret Preparation

To succeed in preparing this recipe, the oil and egg yolks should be at room temperature.
Combine all of the ingredients, except the oil, the hardboiled eggs, and herbs, in a not-too-large bowl and mix well. This is best done with an immersion blender or hand mixer, but a regular whisk will also do the job. My favorite is the immersion blender.

Stir the mixture while slowly but surely adding the oil. If the oil combines with the egg yolks, then all is going well. If not, add the oil more slowly.

If the mixture is too thick, then simply mix in some water. By adding some vinegar at the end, the mayonnaise will become somewhat thicker and also lighter in color. Finally, add the finely-chopped hardboiled eggs and the chopped herbs.

ALABAMA WHISKEY MAYONNAISE

It is really the classic cocktail sauce and, therefore, goes well with shrimp, prawns, lobster, and poultry.

The whiskey can of course be replaced with cognac, calvados, or rum. For all of those who like it classic...

Ingredients

Makes 1½ cups (300 g)

2 egg yolks
2 tsp. mustard
¼-½ tsp Worcester Sauce
2 tsp. vinegar
1 pinch of salt
¼ tsp. sugar
About 1 cup (250 g) oil
3-4 tbsp. ketchup
4-6 tbsp. whiskey

Secret Preparation

To succeed in preparing this recipe, the oil and egg yolks should be at room temperature.

Combine all of the ingredients, except the oil, ketchup, and whiskey, in a not-too-large bowl and mix well. This is best done with an immersion blender or hand mixer, but a regular whisk will also do the job. My favorite is the immersion blender.

Stir the mixture while slowly but surely adding the oil. If the oil combines with the egg yolks, then all is going well. If not, add the oil more slowly.

If the mixture is too thick, then simply mix in some water. By adding some vinegar at the end, the mayonnaise will become somewhat thicker and also lighter in color.

Stir in both the ketchup and whiskey at the end.